IMAGININGS

Reading Between the Lines of Bible Stories

by

Bud Ross

Copyright © 2012 by Bud Ross

Imaginings
by Bud Ross

Printed in the United States of America

ISBN 9781622300235

All rights reserved solely by the author. The author guarantees all contents are original and do not infringe upon the legal rights of any other person or work. No part of this book may be reproduced in any form without the permission of the author. The views expressed in this book are not necessarily those of the publisher.

Unless otherwise indicated, Bible quotations are taken from the New Living Translation. Copyright © 2007 by Tyndale House Publishers, Inc.; New International Version, Copyright © 2011, by Biblica.

www.xulonpress.com

Dedicated to Judy, the best thing that ever happened to me

TABLE OF CONTENTS

Introduction vii

Guess Who's Coming To Church 9

It's Not The How; It's The Who 17

Baby Shower At The Nursing Home 23

Of Pits And Palaces 28

Possessed! 33

Exorcism 101 38

Living In Your Element 44

The Sinner's Hospital 49

What's The Big Deal About Jesus Being Tempted? 54

Fish Tales 59

Bird Brains 66

A Tale Of Two Prophets 70

Bent Out Of Shape 74

Epilogue 79

INTRODUCTION

Elisha prayed, *"'Open his eyes, Lord, so that he may see.' Then the Lord opened the servant's eyes, and he looked and saw the hills full of horses and chariots of fire all around Elisha"* (2 Kings 6:17). What might we see in familiar Scripture if we were to make the same request for our own eyes?

If you pull the Scriptures through the knothole of your own imagination, how might they come to life? What might happen if you asked questions of Scripture like, What was the weather like? How big was the crowd? What did his face look like when he said that? What long-term effect did the event have? What happened when Bible characters compared notes? What is the story supposed to mean to a twenty-first-century, postmodern person? One thing is certain, **there is more in Scripture than meets the eye**.

Remember the words of Jesus: *"Blessed are your eyes because they see"* (Matt. 13:16).

Bud Ross

GUESS WHO'S COMING TO CHURCH

SCRIPTURE

One of the Pharisees asked Jesus to have dinner with him, so Jesus went to his home and sat down to eat. When a certain immoral woman from that city heard he was eating there, she brought a beautiful alabaster jar filled with expensive perfume. Then she knelt behind him at his feet, weeping. Her tears fell on his feet, and she wiped them off with her hair. Then she kept kissing his feet and putting perfume on them.

When the Pharisee who had invited him saw this, he said to himself, "If this man were a prophet, he would know what kind of woman is touching him. She's a sinner!"

Then Jesus answered his thoughts. "Simon," he said to the Pharisee, "I have something to say to you."

"Go ahead, Teacher," Simon replied.

Then Jesus told him this story: "A man loaned money to two people—500 pieces of silver to one and 50 pieces to the other. But neither of them could repay him, so he kindly forgave them both, canceling their debts. Who do you suppose loved him more after that?"

Simon answered, "I suppose the one for whom he canceled the larger debt."

"That's right," Jesus said. Then he turned to the woman and said to Simon, "Look at this woman kneeling here. When I entered your home, you didn't offer me water to wash the dust from my feet, but she has washed them with her tears and wiped them with her hair. You didn't greet me with a kiss, but from the time I first came in, she has not stopped kissing my feet. You neglected the courtesy of olive oil to anoint my head, but she has anointed my feet with rare perfume.

"I tell you, her sins—and they are many—have been forgiven, so she has shown me much love. But a person who is forgiven little shows only little love." Then Jesus said to the woman, "Your sins are forgiven."

The men at the table said among themselves, "Who is this man, that he goes around forgiving sins?"

And Jesus said to the woman, "Your faith has saved you; go in peace."

Luke 7:36-50

~ ~ ~ ~ ~

Eventually he came to the Samaritan village of Sychar, near the field that Jacob gave to his son Joseph. Jacob's well was there; and Jesus, tired from the long walk, sat wearily beside the well about noontime. Soon a Samaritan woman came to draw water, and Jesus said to her, "Please give me a drink." He was alone at the time because his disciples had gone into the village to buy some food.

The woman was surprised, for Jews refuse to have anything to do with Samaritans. She said to Jesus, "You are a Jew, and I am a Samaritan woman. Why are you asking me for a drink?"

Jesus replied, "If you only knew the gift God has for you and who you are speaking to, you would ask me, and I would give you living water."

"But sir, you don't have a rope or a bucket," she said, "and this well is very deep. Where would you get this living water? And besides, do you think you're greater than our ancestor Jacob, who gave us this well? How can you offer better water than he and his sons and his animals enjoyed?"

Jesus replied, "Anyone who drinks this water will soon become thirsty again. But those who drink the water I give will never be thirsty again. It becomes a fresh, bubbling spring within them, giving them eternal life."

"Please, sir," the woman said, "give me this water! Then I'll never be thirsty again, and I won't have to come here to get water."

"Go and get your husband," Jesus told her.

"I don't have a husband," the woman replied.

Jesus said, "You're right! You don't have a husband— for you have had five husbands, and you aren't even married to the man you're living with now. You certainly spoke the truth!"

"Sir," the woman said, "you must be a prophet. So tell me, why is it that you Jews insist that Jerusalem is the only place of worship, while we Samaritans claim it is here at Mount Gerizim, where our ancestors worshiped?"

Jesus replied, "Believe me, dear woman, the time is coming when it will no longer matter whether you worship the Father on this mountain or in Jerusalem. You Samaritans know very little about the one you worship, while we Jews know all about him, for salvation comes through the Jews. But the time is coming—indeed it's here now—when true worshipers will worship the Father in spirit and in truth. The Father is looking for those who will worship him that way. For God is Spirit, so those who worship him must worship in spirit and in truth."

The woman said, "I know the Messiah is coming—the one who is called Christ. When he comes, he will explain everything to us."

Then Jesus told her, "I AM the Messiah!"

John 4:5-26

~ ~ ~ ~ ~

Early the next morning he was back again at the Temple. A crowd soon gathered, and he sat down and taught them. As he was speaking, the teachers of religious law and the Pharisees brought a woman who had been caught in the act of adultery. They put her in front of the crowd.

"Teacher," they said to Jesus, "this woman was caught in the act of adultery. The law of Moses says to stone her. What do you say?"

They were trying to trap him into saying something they could use against him, but Jesus stooped down and wrote in the dust with his finger. They kept demanding an answer, so he stood up again and said, "All right, but let the one who has never sinned throw the first stone!" Then he stooped down again and wrote in the dust.

When the accusers heard this, they slipped away one by one, beginning with the oldest, until only Jesus was left in the middle of the crowd with the woman. Then Jesus stood up again and said to the woman, "Where are your accusers? Didn't even one of them condemn you?"

"No, Lord," she said.

And Jesus said, "Neither do I. Go and sin no more."

John 8:2-11

~ ~ ~ ~ ~

IMAGINE

"a certain immoral woman" – Luke 7:37

"You have had five husbands" – John 4:18

". . . a woman who had been caught in the act of adultery" – John 8:3

~ ~ ~ ~ ~

Three women with embarrassing pasts. Three women who each encountered the gracious presence of Jesus. What if all three women were among the three thousand baptized at Pentecost? What if all three attended worship together the following Sunday? What if they became acquainted through the proximity of worship? It might have happened something like this.

It had been seven days since she felt the refreshing cleansing of his blood washing away her lifetime of guilt—seven days since she and three thousand others had felt their souls infused with the Spirit's power. Timidly entering the place of worship, her eyes traveled across the imposing room, searching for an inconspicuous place to sit. She couldn't escape the feeling that a person with her past didn't belong in a room full of saints. Then she saw it—a seat near the back, in the shadows where another worshipper sat alone, her eyes examining the limestone floor.

Cautiously she approached the vacant seat, her long hair bracketing an empty alabaster flask on a silver chain around her neck. She flinched at the noise her shoes made on the stone floor. She feared attracting any attention to herself. Shifting her weight to the front of her shoes, she silently approached the inconspicuous bench. The seat would barely accommodate two worshippers. As she made eye contact with the other silent worshipper, she thought she saw a look of uncertainty in her eyes, a look that said, "Like you, I don't feel I belong here." Risking rejection, she whispered, "Is it all right for someone like me to sit here?" With a faint smile the other woman replied, "I was just about to ask you the same thing. I'm a five-time divorcee, and I don't know if divorced people are welcome here." With a breath of relief, the longhaired woman whispered, "If they let a former prostitute like me attend, they will surely welcome a divorcee." The divorcee spread a smile of relief and grasped her new sister's hand in friendship.

Both women were stunned when the woman in front of them turned around, her eyes mirroring a kindred spirit. Her hand joined theirs. "I don't mean to eavesdrop, but you have no idea how relieved I am to hear your stories. I was being unfaithful to my husband with another man when I got caught. I was dragged naked, kicking and screaming, before a religious mob that planned to stone me. I was humiliated and terrified as I stood in front of those angry men, whose white-knuckled hands held sharp-edged rocks. When they asked Jesus his opinion about how I should be punished, he kneeled and wrote in the sand. I remember the relief I felt when all eyes turned from me to try to see what he was writing. That was my first experience with grace. When my accusers left, I had my second experience with grace, when he spoke to me with compassion and forgiveness."

The longhaired woman reminisced, "He told me, 'Your sins are forgiven.'" Her friend seated beside her added, "He told me I would become a spring, giving the water of eternal life to others."

Together they had made the great discovery—the church is a hospital for sinners, not a museum for saints. On that first Sunday as they worshipped together, they didn't know church was a gathering place for kindred spirits. They just knew the weight of guilt had been lifted and they were there to honor the one who did the lifting.

So might have begun house church number one in the church at Jerusalem. The three women didn't live happily ever after, but happily they lived ever after.

~ ~ ~ ~ ~

FOOD FOR THOUGHT

Which of the three women had the most embarrassing past?

What can be generalized about sexual sin from the way Jesus responded to the three women?

How can a church facilitate support for people who have had similar struggles with sin and guilt?

How can a church practically implement James's admonition, "Confess your sins to one another" (James 5:16)?

Describe Jesus' technique for accepting the sinner without condoning the sin.

~ ~ ~ ~ ~

SHARING IT WITH GOD

God of sinners and saints, thank you for accepting me. Cleanse my heart of my guilt, and empower me to live a pure life. Give me the same accepting spirit toward others that your Son had. Embolden me to share my weaknesses with those who would be strengthened by the sharing. Amen.

IT'S NOT THE HOW; IT'S THE WHO

SCRIPTURE

Then they reached Jericho, and as Jesus and his disciples left town, a large crowd followed him. A blind beggar named Bartimaeus (son of Timaeus) was sitting beside the road. When Bartimaeus heard Jesus of Nazareth was nearby, he began to shout, "Jesus, Son of David, have mercy on me!"

"Be quiet!" many of the people yelled at him.

But he only shouted louder, "Son of David, have mercy on me!"

When Jesus heard him, he stopped and said, "Tell him to come here."

So they called the blind man. "Cheer up," they said. "Come on, he's calling you!" Bartimaeus threw aside his coat, jumped up, and came to Jesus.

"What do you want me to do for you?" Jesus asked.

"My rabbi," the blind man said, "I want to see!"

And Jesus said to him, "Go, for your faith has healed you." Instantly the man could see, and he followed Jesus down the road.

Mark 10:46-53

~ ~ ~ ~ ~

IMAGININGS

After Jesus left the girl's home, two blind men followed along behind him, shouting, "Son of David, have mercy on us!"

They went right into the house where he was staying, and Jesus asked them, "Do you believe I can make you see?"

"Yes, Lord," they told him, "we do."

Then he touched their eyes and said, "Because of your faith, it will happen." Then their eyes were opened, and they could see! Jesus sternly warned them, "Don't tell anyone about this."

Matthew 9:27-30

~ ~ ~ ~ ~

When they arrived at Bethsaida, some people brought a blind man to Jesus, and they begged him to touch the man and heal him. Jesus took the blind man by the hand and led him out of the village. Then, spitting on the man's eyes, he laid his hands on him and asked, "Can you see anything now?"

The man looked around. "Yes," he said, "I see people, but I can't see them very clearly. They look like trees walking around."

Then Jesus placed his hands on the man's eyes again, and his eyes were opened. His sight was completely restored, and he could see everything clearly.

Mark 8:22-25

~ ~ ~ ~ ~

As Jesus was walking along, he saw a man who had been blind from birth. "Rabbi," his disciples asked him, "why was this man born blind? Was it because of his own sins or his parents' sins?"

"It was not because of his sins or his parents' sins," Jesus

IMAGININGS

answered. "This happened so the power of God could be seen in him. We must quickly carry out the tasks assigned us by the one who sent us. The night is coming, and then no one can work. But while I am here in the world, I am the light of the world."

Then he spit on the ground, made mud with the saliva, and spread the mud over the blind man's eyes. He told him, "Go wash yourself in the pool of Siloam" (Siloam means "sent"). So the man went and washed and came back seeing!

John 9:1-7

~ ~ ~ ~ ~

IMAGINE

"'Go for your faith has healed you.' Instantly the man could see." – Mark 10:52

"He touched their eyes. . . and they could see!"
– Matthew 9:29-30

". . . spitting on the man's eyes . . . Jesus placed his hands on the man's eyes again . . . and he could see everything clearly." – Mark 8:23-25

"He spit on the ground, made mud with the saliva, and spread the mud over the blind man's eyes. He told him, 'Go wash yourself in the pool of Siloam'. So the man went and washed and came back seeing." – John 9:6-7

~ ~ ~ ~ ~

Four blind men were given sight through the compassion and power of Jesus. The manner in which Jesus healed each of them was amazingly varied. What if the four formerly blind men had engaged in a discussion of how Jesus heals. It might have gone something like this.

My name is Bartimaeus. I'll never forget that day I sat by the roadside begging. I know you three understand the humiliation of a dependent lifestyle. Little did I know this was the day I would meet Jesus and everything would change. When my friends said Jesus wanted me to come to him, I threw off my cloak, sprang up, and hurried to where he was. I didn't care if I tripped or ran into someone. I just wanted to get to Jesus as quickly as possible. When I finally bumped into him with my outstretched arms, he asked me the very question I hoped he would ask: what did I want him to do for me? Without pause I answered, "I want to see." He spoke, and instantly I could see. Just that quickly, I could see!

Listening carefully, the second man who had been healed of blindness spoke: *"There were two of us who shared the companionship of blindness, and we were both healed at the same time. We had heard about his recent miracles, healing a paralyzed man and a hemorrhaging woman and even raising the dead, so we had high antennas for any news of him being in our neighborhood. When we heard he had raised a girl from the dead, we latched on to a friend who was following him so that we could stay within earshot, and we began yelling, begging for his help. When he entered a house, we stumbled in right behind him, determined to receive his healing power. Bartimaeus, I don't mean to be argumentative, but you left out the most important part of how Jesus heals blindness. After he spoke to us, he touched our eyes, and then we could see. I don't know how you could forget the touch, Bartimaeus."*

Bartimaeus countered, *"Touch? There was no touch! When Jesus heals blindness, he just speaks it away."*

IMAGININGS

Interrupting the debate, a third newly sighted man spoke: *"You are both wrong. When Jesus came to Bethsaida, some friends of mine, understanding the necessity of touch, took me to Jesus so that he could touch me and heal me. But that's the point at which you both seem to have some memory lapse. First, he leads you out of town, then he spits on your eyes, then he touches you, and you can see a little bit. Then he touches you a second time, and you can see clearly. That, my memory-challenged friends, is how Jesus heals blindness—touch, spit, touch again!"*

Bartimaeus continued to insist that healing comes by command alone, without touch. The second recipient of healing insisted it is command plus a single touch that heals. And the man from Bethsaida adamantly insisted on five steps in the plan of healing: lead, speak, spit, touch, and touch again.

The fourth man had grown increasingly irritated at the forgetfulness of his three friends and couldn't stand to sit in silence any longer. He interrupted the debate with what he was certain was the correct answer, which they all had overlooked: *"You are all wrong. Being blind from birth, I know more about blindness than any of you. You are forgetting the crucial element in healing blindness—mud! I remember clearly his healing technique. When Jesus heals blindness, he doesn't just speak the blindness away or just touch it away or just use saliva to remove the darkness. He makes mud with his saliva, smears the mud on your eyes, and then has you wash in the pool of Siloam. You can't forget the mud! No mud, no healing!*

And so might have begun the first four denominations: The "Mudites," the "Anti-Mudites," the "Touch-Me's" and the "Touch-Me Nots." How grateful we should be that when the blind man in John 9 was asked about his healing, he simply replied, *"All I know is that I used to be blind, but now I can see!"(v. 25).*

~ ~ ~ ~ ~

FOOD FOR THOUGHT

In what ways does Christendom behave like the four blind men in our imaginary story?

What is the effect when unbelievers see churches arguing over "the how" rather than "the who"?

Why did Jesus use different techniques for healing blindness?

Is denominationalism a good thing?

Is denominationalism a necessary thing?

~ ~ ~ ~ ~

SHARING IT WITH GOD

God who gives sight to the blind, increase my vision. Help me to see you clearly pictured in your Word. Help me to see you in the face of your Son. Remove the astigmatism that keeps me from focusing on your will for my life. Help me to be nearsighted about my own shortcomings and farsighted about the shortcomings of others. Amen.

~ ~ ~ ~ ~

BABY SHOWER AT THE NURSING HOME

Scripture

The LORD appeared again to Abraham near the oak grove belonging to Mamre. One day Abraham was sitting at the entrance to his tent during the hottest part of the day. He looked up and noticed three men standing nearby. When he saw them, he ran to meet them and welcomed them, bowing low to the ground.

"My lord," he said, "if it pleases you, stop here for a while. Rest in the shade of this tree while water is brought to wash your feet. And since you've honored your servant with this visit, let me prepare some food to refresh you before you continue on your journey."

"All right," they said. "Do as you have said."

So Abraham ran back to the tent and said to Sarah, "Hurry! Get three large measures of your best flour, knead it into dough, and bake some bread." Then Abraham ran out to the herd and chose a tender calf and gave it to his servant, who quickly prepared it. When the food was ready, Abraham took some yogurt and milk and the roasted meat, and he served it to the men. As they ate, Abraham waited on them in the shade of the trees.

"Where is Sarah, your wife?" the visitors asked.

"She's inside the tent," Abraham replied.

Then one of them said, "I will return to you about this time next year, and your wife, Sarah, will have a son!"

Sarah was listening to this conversation from the tent. Abraham and Sarah were both very old by this time, and Sarah was long past the age of having children. So she laughed silently to herself and said, "How could a worn-out woman like me enjoy such pleasure, especially when my master—my husband—is also so old?"

Then the LORD said to Abraham, "Why did Sarah laugh? Why did she say, 'Can an old woman like me have a baby?' Is anything too hard for the LORD? I will return about this time next year, and Sarah will have a son."

Sarah was afraid, so she denied it, saying, "I didn't laugh."

But the LORD said, "No, you did laugh."

Genesis 18:1-15

~ ~ ~ ~ ~

IMAGINE

"Is anything too hard for the Lord?" – Genesis 18:14

~ ~ ~ ~ ~

Sixty-five-year-old women have a hard time riding camels. Just getting on the critter is a challenge. But when you are the wife of a seventy-five-year-old Bedouin who has wanderlust in his veins, you do what you have to do. Their journey may have started something like this.

The gentleman in Abram caused him to kneel and offer his knee as a step to his gray-headed wife, as she climbed

IMAGININGS

onto her camel. If Abram had faith in God, Sarai had faith in Abram. With few possessions and no map, she rode off into the sunset, leaving behind friends and family. "At least now," she thought, "he may get that 'Let's have a baby' obsession out of his mind. Surely he will be content to live out his days just traveling to see what's over the next sand dune."

Once they were mounted on their camels, Abram gave the command, "Let's go!" When she asked him why they were leaving, he just said, "God said to." "Just like a man," she thought, "making a major decision about where we will live without even consulting the little woman." She asked, "Which god told you to leave? The sun god? The moon god? Maybe the god of the sand dunes?" The man of few words simply replied, "God."

A few years into their nomadic journey, she began to notice a pattern to their lives. People who treated them well prospered. People who treated them poorly suffered. Consider the time Pharaoh came courting. Why in the world didn't Abram defend her honor? It was flattering to be courted at her age, but it was wrong to be courted when you were married to another. Pharaoh would soon learn that those who treat Abram poorly suffer greatly. No sooner had he taken Sarai into his house than they came in swarms—the plagues: huge, horrible, debilitating plagues on Pharaoh and his family. When the plagues hit, Sarai remembered something Abram told her about God's promise to "curse those who curse you." Just the opposite was also true. For instance, Abram's nephew, Lot, always treated Abram with respect; and when Abram became rich, so did Lot. When she was around Lot, she was reminded of the rest of that promise to Abram, the promise that God would "bless those who bless you." She was beginning to feel that this God of Abram's was very "hands-on." It was a secure feeling.

Since riding off into the sunset on the back of a loping camel, Sarai's life had been full of wonderful serendipities: riches, land, friends, and a loving husband whose "God-can-do" spirit was contagious. What a life! *Then the rabbit died!* It couldn't be true! Pregnant? At age ninety? She laughed a lot for the next nine months. This was not the skeptical laughter she guffawed earlier when she was expected to believe she could have a baby in her old age. This laughter was joyous. She laughed at the prospect of hobbling with her cane into her baby shower. She laughed when she imagined how appropriate it would be if someone gave walkers to both her and the baby. She laughed now that she realized her precious boy was the answer to God's question, "Is anything too hard for the Lord?"

Every day as she looked at her giggling baby the now renamed Sarah laughed in joy and smiled in faith. She invited all her friends over to laugh with her.

~ ~ ~ ~ ~

FOOD FOR THOUGHT

What concerns might a ninety-year-old woman have about being pregnant?

How might the other women around Sarah react to her pregnancy?

Much has been made of Abraham's faith in leaving his roots and going where God directed. How would you describe Sarah's faith?

What examples can you think of during the travels of Abraham and Sarah of God blessing those who blessed them and cursing those who cursed them?

What experiences have you had that taught you the truth Sarah learned: "Is anything too hard for the Lord?"

~ ~ ~ ~ ~

SHARING IT WITH GOD

God of Abraham and Sarah, increase my faith to believe in the impossible. Keep me from imposing my limitations on You. Stretch my horizons so that I may see your big picture rather than my tiny one. Deepen my well so that I might drink from your aquifer rather than from my shallow pool. Open my heart so I may sense your constant empowerment to do what you have directed me to do. Keep me from being afraid to believe. Amen.

~ ~ ~ ~ ~

OF PITS AND PALACES

SCRIPTURE

So Jacob settled again in the land of Canaan, where his father had lived as a foreigner.

This is the account of Jacob and his family. When Joseph was seventeen years old, he often tended his father's flocks. He worked for his half brothers, the sons of his father's wives Bilhah and Zilpah. But Joseph reported to his father some of the bad things his brothers were doing.

Jacob loved Joseph more than any of his other children because Joseph had been born to him in his old age. So one day Jacob had a special gift made for Joseph—a beautiful robe. But his brothers hated Joseph because their father loved him more than the rest of them. They couldn't say a kind word to him.

One night Joseph had a dream, and when he told his brothers about it, they hated him more than ever. "Listen to this dream," he said. "We were out in the field, tying up bundles of grain. Suddenly my bundle stood up, and your bundles all gathered around and bowed low before mine!"

His brothers responded, "So you think you will be our king, do you? Do you actually think you will reign over us?" And they hated him all the more because of his dreams and

IMAGININGS

the way he talked about them.

Soon Joseph had another dream, and again he told his brothers about it. "Listen, I have had another dream," he said. "The sun, moon, and eleven stars bowed low before me!"

This time he told the dream to his father as well as to his brothers, but his father scolded him. "What kind of dream is that?" he asked. "Will your mother and I and your brothers actually come and bow to the ground before you?" But while his brothers were jealous of Joseph, his father wondered what the dreams meant.

Soon after this, Joseph's brothers went to pasture their father's flocks at Shechem. When they had been gone for some time, Jacob said to Joseph, "Your brothers are pasturing the sheep at Shechem. Get ready, and I will send you to them."

"I'm ready to go," Joseph replied.

"Go and see how your brothers and the flocks are getting along," Jacob said. "Then come back and bring me a report." So Jacob sent him on his way, and Joseph traveled to Shechem from their home in the valley of Hebron.

When he arrived there, a man from the area noticed him wandering around the countryside. "What are you looking for?" he asked.

Genesis 37:1-15

~ ~ ~ ~ ~

Since Joseph was governor of all Egypt and in charge of selling grain to all the people, it was to him that his brothers came. When they arrived, they bowed before him with their faces to the ground.

Genesis 42:6

~ ~ ~ ~ ~

IMAGINE

"Do you actually think you will reign over us?"
– Genesis 37:8

"Do you really believe that your mother, your brothers, and I will bow down to you?" *–Genesis 37:10*

~ ~ ~ ~ ~

God answers prayer in one of three ways: "yes," "no" and "later." We are thrilled with "yes" and accustomed to an occasional "no," but it's the "later" answer that gives us angst. When God twice revealed to Joseph in dreams that he would be preeminent over his brothers, a teenaged Joseph struggled with his ego and flaunted the dream to his brothers. The chain of events that unfolded in Joseph's life must have driven him to his knees, praying repeatedly for the fulfillment of God's promise. Few people have ever received the dreaded "later" answer more than the Hebrew patriarch, Joseph. What if his prayer journey went something like this.

As a teen, the longing of Joseph's heart (aka prayer) is for his brothers to acknowledge his preeminence over them. When he flaunts his special favorite-son coat, his brothers throw him into a pit. Instantly, his prayer for preeminence is put on hold and replaced by, *"Lord, get me out of this pit."* God's answer comes a few hours later when Joseph is lifted out of the pit. But, disappointingly, he is delivered not to the prominent position he so cherished but to a slave trader's wagon.

The prayer for preeminence remains on hold while Joseph prays for deliverance from the slave traders. God's answer comes a few days later, when Joseph is delivered

IMAGININGS

from the slave traders, but again the answer is not the one Joseph wants. The disappointing answers to Joseph's prayers continue when he is sold as a slave to Potiphar. Things go well in Potiphar's house, until Mrs. Potiphar becomes enamored with Joseph. Joseph's prayer for preeminence over his brothers is now all but forgotten, as he prays for deliverance from Mrs. Potiphar's seductive overtures. Again his prayer is answered with "later." This time God's answer is delayed for eleven years. Over a decade after his prayer for deliverance, Joseph is finally delivered from slavery, but not to the destiny of his choice. Mrs. Potiphar's trumped-up charge lands him in prison. Not only did his prayer receive the unwanted "later" answer, but when the "later" morphs into "yes," it's still not the answer Joseph wants.

From his new home in a prison cell, Joseph's long-ago offered prayer for preeminence has become just a fading memory. Of much greater concern now is getting an answer to a new prayer, a prayer for deliverance from prison. Again the answer is "later." Only after two more years does the prayer for deliverance finally receive a "yes," when Joseph is promoted to second in command in Egypt. The two-year delay is another strong reminder to Joseph that when God answers our prayers with "later," it does not mean "never."

From the pit to the palace! It's been twenty-two years since Joseph was thrown into the pit. Twenty-two years since he was so hungry for preeminence over his brothers. Twenty-two years of God saying, "Later." Finally, the day arrives when "later" becomes "yes." *"And Joseph's brothers came and bowed themselves before him with their faces to the ground."* Who knew that preeminence would be given, not to satisfy Joseph's ego but to save his family from starvation? Who knew that the twenty-two-year delay in Joseph's preeminence would result in blessing for all of Israel?

Whether our prayers are offered from the pit or the palace, from Potiphar's house or a prison cell, God still hears, and he still answers: "yes," "no" or "later."

~ ~ ~ ~ ~

FOOD FOR THOUGHT

To which of your current prayers does the answer appear to be, "Later"?

In hindsight, what unexpected blessings came to your life from one of God's "later" answers to your prayer?

As Joseph took a twenty-year journey from the pit to the palace, what options did he have concerning his view of God?

Of all Joseph's disappointments in life, which might have been the most challenging to his faith?

Of all your disappointments in life, which is the most challenging to your faith?

~ ~ ~ ~ ~

SHARING IT WITH GOD

God with whom a day is like a thousand years and a thousand years is like a day, help me look to you rather than the clock and the calendar. Keep me from assigning my time limits to you. Increase my faith to believe that "Later" from you is better than "Yes" from the enemy. Help me to believe that in your good time you work all things for good. Amen.

~ ~ ~ ~ ~

POSSESSED!

SCRIPTURE

About eight days later Jesus took Peter, John, and James up on a mountain to pray. And as he was praying, the appearance of his face was transformed, and his clothes became dazzling white. Suddenly, two men, Moses and Elijah, appeared and began talking with Jesus. They were glorious to see. And they were speaking about his exodus from this world, which was about to be fulfilled in Jerusalem.

Peter and the others had fallen asleep. When they woke up, they saw Jesus' glory and the two men standing with him. As Moses and Elijah were starting to leave, Peter, not even knowing what he was saying, blurted out, "Master, it's wonderful for us to be here! Let's make three shelters as memorials—one for you, one for Moses, and one for Elijah." But even as he was saying this, a cloud overshadowed them, and terror gripped them as the cloud covered them.

Then a voice from the cloud said, "This is my Son, my Chosen One. Listen to him." When the voice finished, Jesus was there alone. They didn't tell anyone at that time what they had seen.

The next day, after they had come down the mountain, a large crowd met Jesus. A man in the crowd called out to him, "Teacher, I beg you to look at my son, my only child. An evil spirit keeps seizing him, making him scream. It throws him

IMAGININGS

into convulsions so that he foams at the mouth. It batters him and hardly ever leaves him alone. I begged your disciples to cast out the spirit, but they couldn't do it."

Jesus said, "You faithless and corrupt people! How long must I be with you and put up with you?" Then he said to the man, "Bring your son here."

As the boy came forward, the demon knocked him to the ground and threw him into a violent convulsion. But Jesus rebuked the evil spirit and healed the boy. Then he gave him back to his father. Awe gripped the people as they saw this majestic display of God's power.

While everyone was marveling at everything he was doing, Jesus said to his disciples, "Listen to me and remember what I say. The Son of Man is going to be betrayed into the hands of his enemies." But they didn't know what he meant. Its significance was hidden from them, so they couldn't understand it, and they were afraid to ask him about it.

Then his disciples began arguing about which of them was the greatest.

Luke 9:28-46

~ ~ ~ ~ ~

IMAGINE

"Jesus ordered the demon to stop." – Luke 9:42

~ ~ ~ ~ ~

Havilah watched the smoke spiral into the sky, as he burned the stubble from his field to prepare for next spring's planting. Then he heard the screams. He turned and, to his horror, saw his little boy wallowing in the flames, his clothes beginning to smolder. Scorching his own hands, he beat the flames out and carried his screaming child into the

IMAGININGS

house. Together with his wife, Adah, they gently removed the clothing from the terrified child, exposing the scars from previous burns. They were fortunate this time. Havilah heard the screams before the fire burned through the child's clothing. Being burned alive was a constant threat with demon possession. Compounding the horrific fear of their child being burned to death was the realization that nobody knew what to do about demon possession. There were no known cures. There were only shallow superstitions that usually put the possessed person through additional misery. Some families forced horrible potions down the throats of protesting victims. Others, in desperation, chained the possessed ones to trees so the rest of the family could go about their daily duties.

In desperation Havilah took his child to a small group of Jesus' followers, who reportedly had had some limited success casting out demons. But in spite of his pleading and their best efforts, the child remained under the control of Satan. Havilah was a proud man and not accustomed to begging, but this was his child, his only child, and he would pay any price to find a cure for his little boy. So he begged. The Jesus followers tried, but even as they commanded the demon to come out, the low guttural sound of an impending episode began rumbling from the small boy's throat.

As the child's seizure began, a crowd of people was gathering near the base of a nearby mountain. Rumor had it that Jesus was making an appearance. In absolute desperation, Havilah ran to Jesus and again unashamedly begged for deliverance for his son. As he spoke, the demon violently threw the boy to the ground, seizing him with excruciating convulsions.

With the speed of a lightning bolt from heaven, Jesus

took charge of the situation. In one breath he commanded the demon to leave the child, and in the next breath he healed the boy. With overwhelming joy Havilah and Adah held their precious child and stroked his new, unscarred skin. They smelled the sweetness of his demonless breath and ran their fingers through his previously matted hair. They had their son back!

~ ~ ~ ~ ~

FOOD FOR THOUGHT

What are some twenty-first-century versions of demon possession?

What is the value of attributing some out-of-control behaviors to the presence of Satan in a person's life?

How can one tell if he or she is depending on people rather than Jesus for solutions to life's greatest problems?

How do families today react to a "possessed" family member?

At what point in a loved one's "possession" would you turn to Jesus for help?

Is there an area of concern in your life where "you have not because you ask not"(James 4:2)?

~ ~ ~ ~ ~

SHARING IT WITH GOD

Great Physician who is not threatened by the worst hell

can offer, increase my faith in your ability to meet my deepest needs. Keep me from surrendering to Satan's great allurements. Cast from me that which hinders my spiritual growth. May your Holy Spirit fill the void in my life where Satan has been cast out. Thank you for letting me be on the winning side of the great war with Satan. Amen.

~ ~ ~ ~ ~

EXORCISM 101

SCRIPTURE

One day Jesus called together his twelve disciples and gave them power and authority to cast out all demons and to heal all diseases. Then he sent them out to tell everyone about the Kingdom of God and to heal the sick. "Take nothing for your journey," he instructed them. "Don't take a walking stick, a traveler's bag, food, money, or even a change of clothes. Wherever you go, stay in the same house until you leave town. And if a town refuses to welcome you, shake its dust from your feet as you leave to show that you have abandoned those people to their fate."

So they began their circuit of the villages, preaching the Good News and healing the sick.

Luke 9:1-6

~ ~ ~ ~ ~

The Lord now chose seventy-two other disciples and sent them ahead in pairs to all the towns and places he planned to visit. These were his instructions to them: "The harvest is great, but the workers are few. So pray to the Lord who is in charge of the harvest; ask him to send more workers into his fields. Now go, and remember that I am sending you out as lambs among wolves. Don't take any money with you, nor a traveler's bag, nor an extra pair of sandals. And don't stop to greet anyone on the road.

"Whenever you enter someone's home, first say, 'May God's peace be on this house.' If those who live there are peaceful, the blessing will stand; if they are not, the blessing will return to you. Don't move around from home to home. Stay in one place, eating and drinking what they provide. Don't hesitate to accept hospitality, because those who work deserve their pay.

Luke 10:1-7

~ ~ ~ ~ ~

When the seventy-two disciples returned, they joyfully reported to him, "Lord, even the demons obey us when we use your name!"

"Yes," he told them, "I saw Satan fall from heaven like lightning!

Luke 10:17-18

~ ~ ~ ~ ~

IMAGINE

"Jesus gave them power and authority over all demons." – Luke 9:1

"Lord, in your name even the demons submit to us!" – Luke 10:17

~ ~ ~ ~ ~

Twelve apostles and seventy disciples suddenly found themselves with authority over demons. How did such power affect their egos? What tensions developed as a competitive spirit reared its head among the Jesus followers? At what point did they learn the greatest privilege of being a Jesus follower is not our *power over the tempter* but our *place at the table?* It might have happened something like this.

Jesus gives twelve men power over "all" demons and sends them out on a trial run as his ambassadors. They meticulously follow his instructions to live a Spartan lifestyle during their mission. The mission succeeds beyond their wildest imaginations. During their brief mission, they function as demon-exorcising machines! **What privilege! What honor! What power!**

When they return from their mission, Peter, James, and John are given a unique opportunity when they are invited to go up on the mountain with Jesus to pray. **What privilege! What honor! What power!** The prayer retreat turns into an otherworldly experience as Jesus' appearance changes. First, something incredible happens to the way his face looks. Then his clothes change, becoming a dazzling white. Before the shock of those changes in Jesus' appearance wears off, the two most famous miracle workers in Jewish history, Moses and Elijah, appear out of nowhere. As if those spectacular events weren't enough, the privileged three apostles hear the literal voice of God giving them directions.

It's not hard to imagine those three fishermen becoming increasingly convinced of their own importance as they walk down the mountain with Jesus. How excited they must have been as they anticipated telling the other nine apostles about their experiences on the mountain. Convinced of their special place at the top of the apostolic pyramid, the temptation to gloat must have been irresistible when they discovered that during their absence the other nine apostles had failed in their efforts to cast a demon out of a young boy. One of the three privileged apostles might well have said something like, *"A few days ago when the twelve of us went out as ambassadors, we did not fail one time in our efforts to cast out demons. Look what happens when we three special apostles are gone for a brief time. The rest of you lose your power."* In a competitive environment like that, was it any wonder an argument arose among them as to which one of them was the greatest?

It appears the apostles had become *possessed with demon possession*. John speaks for all three of the newly crowned "exorcism experts," when he describes how appalled they were to see someone who was "not one of us" casting out demons (Luke 9:49). With self-appointed authority that sounds like the board of directors of an elitist social club, they tried to stop the unauthorized exorcist. Jesus' comments reveal their myopia, *"Whoever is not against you is for you"* (v. 50). But his words fell on deaf ears that day and, tragically, those words continue to fall on deaf ears today. To hear Jesus' words and accept their truth is to lose all feelings of competition in religion. How often must Jesus long to say to us when we plot to compete with other Jesus followers, *"They are not against you!"*

The apostles were not the only ones around Jesus who were *possessed with demon possession*. Fast-forward to the moment Jesus sends out seventy others as ambassadors with instructions and empowerment similar to what he gave to the apostles earlier. When the seventy return from that mission, they are pumped! They summarize their greatest source of joy, saying, *"Lord, in your name even the demons submit to us!"* Can you smell the sizzling of scorching egos as nine apostles remember their failure to cast out a demon? Will the debate over who is the greatest in the kingdom now be expanded from twelve men to include an additional seventy exorcists?

Jesus acknowledges their joy when he informs them he was watching every success they had out on the mission field. He even gives their success an otherworldly dimension when he comments on what happened in heaven every time they succeeded in their mission on earth: *"I watched Satan fall from heaven like a flash of lightning."* **What privilege! What honor! What power!**

To seventy disciples and twelve apostles whose egos are bursting with pride, Jesus recommends an awareness of what is really significant in kingdom work: *"Do not rejoice at this, that the spirits submit to you, but rejoice that your names are written in heaven."*

~ ~ ~ ~ ~

FOOD FOR THOUGHT

What went wrong when nine of the apostles who had been given power over "all" demons failed to cast out a demon from a young boy?

If you were one of the chosen three who got to go up on the Mount of Transfiguration with Jesus, what would prevent you from developing an egotistical attitude about your privilege?

What possible motives could cause the apostles to attempt to stop a successful exorcist from casting out demons simply because he did not "follow with" them?

After arguing over who is the greatest and hearing Jesus'

chastising words, *"whoever is not against you is for you,"* how should the apostles have reacted when they saw the rejoicing of seventy disciples who had successfully cast out demons?

In your own life, have you ever felt competitive with other religious groups?

Have you ever had to struggle with your own sense of self-importance regarding your work in the kingdom?

~ ~ ~ ~ ~

SHARING IT WITH GOD

God who has all the power, who cast out my guilt and shame, keep me from the temptation of taking credit when you use me to share your message with others. May your Holy Spirit control my spirit when I see others succeed in areas where I have failed. May your kingdom reign in my heart as I invite others to share in the joy of kingdom living. Amen.

~ ~ ~ ~ ~

LIVING IN YOUR ELEMENT

SCRIPTURE

In the beginning God created the heavens and the earth. The earth was formless and empty, and darkness covered the deep waters. And the Spirit of God was hovering over the surface of the waters.

Then God said, "Let there be light," and there was light. And God saw that the light was good. Then he separated the light from the darkness. God called the light "day" and the darkness "night."

And evening passed and morning came, marking the first day.

Then God said, "Let there be a space between the waters, to separate the waters of the heavens from the waters of the earth." And that is what happened. God made this space to separate the waters of the earth from the waters of the heavens. God called the space "sky."

And evening passed and morning came, marking the second day.

Then God said, "Let the waters beneath the sky flow together into one place, so dry ground may appear." And that is what happened. God called the dry ground "land" and the waters "seas." And God saw that it was good. Then

God said, "Let the land sprout with vegetation—every sort of seed-bearing plant, and trees that grow seed-bearing fruit. These seeds will then produce the kinds of plants and trees from which they came." And that is what happened. The land produced vegetation—all sorts of seed-bearing plants, and trees with seed-bearing fruit. Their seeds produced plants and trees of the same kind. And God saw that it was good.

And evening passed and morning came, marking the third day.

Then God said, "Let lights appear in the sky to separate the day from the night. Let them be signs to mark the seasons, days, and years. Let these lights in the sky shine down on the earth." And that is what happened. God made two great lights—the larger one to govern the day, and the smaller one to govern the night. He also made the stars. God set these lights in the sky to light the earth, to govern the day and night, and to separate the light from the darkness. And God saw that it was good.

And evening passed and morning came, marking the fourth day.

Then God said, "Let the waters swarm with fish and other life. Let the skies be filled with birds of every kind." So God created great sea creatures and every living thing that scurries and swarms in the water, and every sort of bird—each producing offspring of the same kind. And God saw that it was good. Then God blessed them, saying, "Be fruitful and multiply. Let the fish fill the seas, and let the birds multiply on the earth."

And evening passed and morning came, marking the fifth day.

Then God said, "Let the earth produce every sort of animal, each producing offspring of the same kind—livestock, small animals that scurry along the ground, and wild animals." And that is what happened. God made all sorts of wild animals, livestock, and small animals, each able to produce offspring of the same kind. And God saw that it was good.

Then God said, "Let us make human beings in our image, to be like us. They will reign over the fish in the sea, the birds in the sky, the livestock, all the wild animals on the earth, and the small animals that scurry along the ground."

Genesis 1:1-26

~ ~ ~ ~ ~

IMAGINE

"Let there be light . . . and there was . . ." – Genesis 1:3

"Let us make man in our image." – Genesis 1:26

~ ~ ~ ~ ~

There is symmetry to the order of creation. On day one, God created light. Three days later, he created the light bearers: sun, moon, and stars. On day two, God created sky and water. Three days later, He created birds and fish. On day three, God created dry land. Three days later, He created land animals and man. For three days, God created elements suitable for what he would create the next three days. Imagine what would have happened if the order of creation were different. If the first thing God created were a fish, where would it swim? If the first thing God created were a bird, where would it fly? If the first thing God created were a man, where would he walk?

Everything was created to function in its element. Fish function in the water. Birds function in the sky. Land animals function on the land.

IMAGININGS

Of all the things God made, only one was created for two elements—man. Man functions not only in a physical element but also in a spiritual element. The creation story makes this "dual elements" point twice. First, when God created man, he changed the formula from, "Let there be . . . and there was . . ." to "Let us create man in our own image." It is being "in God's image" that defines a human being. There is a part of us that is like God—namely, our spirit. It is our spirit that longs to communicate with God's spirit in something called worship.

The second time the creation story makes the point about man being made to function in a spiritual element is when God "breathed into man the breath of life" (Gen. 2:7). To have God's breath fill one's lungs is to have something holy within you. It is the holy within us that longs to come out in worship.

When we allow ourselves to function in our spiritual element, we live whole, fulfilling lives. When we deny our spiritual element, we become lost and lonely.

The words of the old hymn caution us not to put down our roots on the land we call home: *"This world is not my home, I'm just a passing through."* Wise is the person who recognizes that of the two worlds, the physical and the spiritual, only the spiritual is lasting.

~ ~ ~ ~ ~

FOOD FOR THOUGHT

Compare the first three days of creation with the last three days of creation. What is the correlation between the first three days and the last three days?

How do the following statements imply that man is to function not only on the land but also in the spirit?

1. *"Let us make man in our image" (Gen. 1:26).*

2. *"God formed man of the dust of the ground, and breathed into his nostrils the breath of life; and man became a living soul" (Gen. 2:7).*

How does denying one's spiritual element result in loneliness?

What does the creation story tell us about our physical being? Is it as good or worse than our spiritual being, or are the two linked?

Is one aspect of a person's being more important than another?

What light is shed on the relationship between body and spirit by the teaching in 1 Corinthians 6:19 that the believer's body is the temple of the Holy Spirit?

What does "calling" mean to a person whose life is confined to a dead-end job?

~ ~ ~ ~ ~

SHARING IT WITH GOD

God who created me in your image, how honored I am to be a tiny bit like you. Why you chose me for this honor I do not understand, but my lack of understanding does not diminish the honor. Help me to live up to my calling. Increase my appetite for spiritual things. Keep me from doing most of my living on the land and little of it in the spirit. Amen.

~ ~ ~ ~ ~

THE SINNER'S HOSPITAL

SCRIPTURE

Then Jesus went out to the lakeshore again and taught the crowds that were coming to him. As he walked along, he saw Levi son of Alphaeus sitting at his tax collector's booth. "Follow me and be my disciple," Jesus said to him. So Levi got up and followed him.

Later, Levi invited Jesus and his disciples to his home as dinner guests, along with many tax collectors and other disreputable sinners. (There were many people of this kind among Jesus' followers.) But when the teachers of religious law who were Pharisees saw him eating with tax collectors and other sinners, they asked his disciples, "Why does he eat with such scum?"

When Jesus heard this, he told them, "Healthy people don't need a doctor—sick people do. I have come to call not those who think they are righteous, but those who know they are sinners."

Mark 2:13-17

~ ~ ~ ~ ~

IMAGINE

"Levi invited Jesus and his disciples to his home as dinner guests, along with many tax collectors and other disreputable sinners. (There were many people of this kind among Jesus' followers.)" – Mark 2:15

"Healthy people don't need a doctor—sick people do." – Mark 2:17

~ ~ ~ ~ ~

When the tax collector arrived home after another profitable day at his work, his wife asked how his day had gone. He replied, "It was a typical day, except for the news that one of my competitors walked away from a thriving tax collecting business to become an itinerant preacher." His wife asked, "It wasn't by chance, Levi, was it?" "Yes," he answered, "How did you know?" "We got an invitation to a reception at Levi's house in celebration of a change that has occurred in his life. Do you want to go?" "Absolutely I want to go. I'm dying to find out what would make a man walk away from a lucrative business and turn to a life with no obvious source of income."

When they arrived at the reception, the tax collector's wife was surprised to find the reception was actually a banquet. All of her husband's business associates were there, many of whom were known to be extortionists because of the way they ran their tax collecting booths. She had never seen such a large collection of people with tainted reputations. It was the kind of gathering where you kept your purse close to your side. There wasn't a religious person in the bunch, until the Pharisees and teachers of the law showed up. What an intimidating presence they were to her. Their dress was religious. Their talk was religious. They wore on their faces the pained expressions of the obsessively religious. They made her feel like an outcast from God because of her husband's occupation. Their judgmentalism destroyed an occasion for joy for those who had gathered. Their comment to the followers of Jesus was, "Why do you eat and drink with scum?" "Scum"—that's why she never attended their "church." Who wants to go where you are seen as scum?

She was about ready to leave when the rabbi who was Levi's special guest got her attention with one simple reply to those who were criticizing the nonreligious: "Healthy people don't need a doctor—sick people do."

Levi had seen the church as a hospital for sinners and invited all his sick friends to a banquet at his house. He saw the church as a hospital for sinners because he saw himself as a sinner who had found the cure for his sins in Christ and wanted to use his home as a hospital.

Imagine a church with one of those electronic signs each week inviting a specific kind of sinner to church. One Sunday the sign would announce, "Adultery Sunday. Come and learn about God's grace." The next Sunday it would read, "Liar Sunday. Come and experience a life that is all about truth." Another Sunday it would be, "Gossip Sunday. Come and worship with kindred spirits." And another Sunday the sign would say, "Hypocrite Sunday. Two-faced people welcome." Imagine a church asking people to sit with people who have the same kind of sin in their past. Imagine signs on each pew: "Reserved for idolaters." "Reserved for adulterers." "Reserved for male prostitutes." "Reserved for homosexuals." "Reserved for thieves." "Reserved for greedy people." Reserved for drunkards." "Reserved for abusers." "Reserved for those who have cheated people."

Does that sound ludicrous? Listen to Paul's words, which were intended to be read aloud to the church at Corinth: *"Don't you realize that those who do wrong will not inherit the Kingdom of God? Don't fool yourselves. Those who indulge in sexual sin, or who worship idols, or commit adultery, or are male prostitutes, or practice homosexuality, or are thieves, or greedy people, or drunkards, or are abusive, or cheat people—none of these will inherit the Kingdom of God" (1 Cor. 6:9-10).*

The founder of the church declared, *"I have come to call not those who think they are righteous, but those who know they are sinners and need to repent."* The question is, is he calling you?

~ ~ ~ ~ ~

FOOD FOR THOUGHT

What is the significance of there being "many disreputable sinners" among Jesus' followers (Mark 2:15)?

What was the concern of the teachers of the religious law in Mark 2:15? In what context might today's churchgoer express the same concern?

What effect does it have on your life to hear Jesus state his purpose as calling those who "know they are sinners" (Mark 2:17)?

Would you be comfortable attending a church with a membership similar to the one described in 1 Corinthians 6:9-10?

~ ~ ~ ~ ~

SHARING IT WITH GOD

God of those who acknowledge their sickness, heal me. Keep me from seeing my healing as giving me the right to criticize those who have yet to experience such healing. Give me wisdom as I seek to avoid sin and befriend those who don't. Amen.

~ ~ ~ ~ ~

WHAT'S THE BIG DEAL ABOUT JESUS BEING TEMPTED?

SCRIPTURE

Then Jesus was led by the Spirit into the wilderness to be tempted there by the devil. For forty days and forty nights he fasted and became very hungry. During that time the devil came and said to him, "If you are the Son of God, tell these stones to become loaves of bread." But Jesus told him, "No! The Scriptures say, 'People do not live by bread alone, but by every word that comes from the mouth of God.'"

Then the devil took him to the holy city, Jerusalem, to the highest point of the Temple, and said, "If you are the Son of God, jump off! For the Scriptures say, 'He will order his angels to protect you. And they will hold you up with their hands so you won't even hurt your foot on a stone.'" Jesus responded, "The Scriptures also say, 'You must not test the LORD your God.'"

Next the devil took him to the peak of a very high mountain and showed him all the kingdoms of the world and their glory. "I will give it all to you," he said, "if you will kneel

IMAGININGS

down and worship me." "Get out of here, Satan," Jesus told him. "For the Scriptures say, 'You must worship the LORD your God and serve only him.'"

Then the devil went away, and angels came and took care of Jesus.

Matthew 4:1-11

~ ~ ~ ~ ~

IMAGINE

"Jesus was led by the Spirit into the wilderness to be tempted by the devil." – Matthew 4:1

"If you are the Son of God, tell these stones to become bread." – Matthew 4:2

"The devil took him to the holy city and had him stand on the highest point of the temple. 'If you are the Son of God,' he said, 'throw yourself down.'" – Matthew 4:5-6

"The devil took him to a very high mountain and showed him all the kingdoms of the world and their splendor. 'All this I will give you,' he said, 'if you will bow down and worship me.'" – Matthew 4:8-9

~ ~ ~ ~ ~

When Jesus faced the intense temptations of the wilderness, he struggled with the very nature of his mission on planet earth. At stake was the kind of Messiah he would be. Would he be a Messiah whose focus was on economic issues (turning stones to bread)? Would he be a Messiah whose focus was on drawing crowds with sensationalism (jumping from the pinnacle of the temple)? Would he be a Messiah whose focus was on compromise (bowing down to Satan)? Because he put our interests above his own comfort, he resisted those temptations and lived a salvation-focused life. Imagine what life would be like if Jesus had given in to the three temptations he faced in the wilderness.

With his stomach growling its complaints of hunger, Jesus picks up a handful of stones and with a word turns them into delicious hot rolls with butter and strawberry jam. With his stomach satisfied, he can now listen with interest to Satan's suggestion that they reach a compromise about their competition for the hearts of men. "If you will acknowledge my right to a share of this earth, I will leave you alone. No one will know but the two of us. No crown of thorns, no nails, no cross. What harm could it cause?" Not wanting to be nailed to a tree, he accepts the offer and prepares for an interference-free ministry of feeding the hungry and healing the sick. But before he leaves the wilderness, Satan has one more suggestion: "Don't leave here and preach a sermon on the side of the mountain to a bunch of illiterate Jewish peasants with their hands out. Put a little razz-a-ma-tazz in your ministry. Start off by dazzling the entire population of Jerusalem with a dive off the pinnacle of the temple." Leaving the wilderness with a full stomach and knowing his years on this earth will be hassle-free, he floats to the top of the temple and waits for the crowd to gather. When people are so jammed into the temple court that there is scarcely room to move, he leaps into the air, doing a triple back somersault with two and a half twists, and lands safely and gently on his feet. His fame spreads all over the earth quickly, and his days are filled with popularity as he entertains, feeds, and heals everyone on the planet.

In a short time, the world becomes exceedingly sinful in its self-centered pursuit of a God who gives them what they want rather than what they need. The total purpose of life becomes focused on the here and now. No need for heaven. No concern about hell. No reason to work. No reason to be concerned about sin. No need for a Savior.

So, what would be lost if Jesus had given in to the temptations in the wilderness? Everything!

~ ~ ~ ~ ~

FOOD FOR THOUGHT

How would turning stones into bread change the nature of what Jesus came to earth to accomplish?

How would jumping from the pinnacle of the temple change the nature of what Jesus came to earth to accomplish?

How would bowing down to Satan cause Jesus to change the nature of what he came to earth to accomplish?

In what ways are we also tempted to lose our focus on the nature of Christianity by . . .

. . . overemphasizing ministry to people's felt needs?

. . . pursuing sensationalism rather than teaching the gospel?

. . . choosing compromise rather than Jesus' standards?

~ ~ ~ ~ ~

SHARING IT WITH GOD

God who does not lead us into temptation but delivers us from evil, deliver me from the desire to take the easy road over the high road. Instill in my heart a clear vision of what your Son wanted his kingdom to become. Steel my heart from the lure of compromise that Satan flaunts so skillfully. Thy kingdom come in my heart!

~ ~ ~ ~ ~

FISH TALES

SCRIPTURE

Then they took Jonah and threw him overboard, and the raging sea grew calm. At this the men greatly feared the LORD, and they offered a sacrifice to the LORD and made vows to him.

Now the LORD provided a huge fish to swallow Jonah, and Jonah was in the belly of the fish three days and three nights.

From inside the fish Jonah prayed to the LORD his God. He said:

> "In my distress I called to the LORD, and he answered me. From deep in the realm of the dead I called for help, and you listened to my cry. You hurled me into the depths, into the very heart of the seas, and the currents swirled about me; all your waves and breakers swept over me. I said, 'I have been banished from your sight; yet I will look again toward your holy temple.' The engulfing waters threatened me, the deep surrounded me; seaweed was wrapped around my head. To the roots of the mountains I sank down; the earth beneath barred me in forever. But you, LORD my

God, brought my life up from the pit. "When my life was ebbing away, I remembered you, LORD, and my prayer rose to you, to your holy temple. "Those who cling to worthless idols turn away from God's love for them. But I, with shouts of grateful praise, will sacrifice to you. What I have vowed I will make good. I will say, 'Salvation comes from the LORD.'"

Jonah 1:15–2:10

~ ~ ~ ~ ~

After Jesus and his disciples arrived in Capernaum, the collectors of the two-drachma temple tax came to Peter and asked, "Doesn't your teacher pay the temple tax?"

"Yes, he does," he replied.

When Peter came into the house, Jesus was the first to speak. "What do you think, Simon?" he asked. "From whom do the kings of the earth collect duty and taxes—from their own children or from others?"

"From others," Peter answered.

"Then the children are exempt," Jesus said to him. "But so that we may not cause offense, go to the lake and throw out your line. Take the first fish you catch; open its mouth and you will find a four-drachma coin. Take it and give it to them for my tax and yours."

Matthew 17:24-27

~ ~ ~~ ~

Jesus called his disciples to him and said, "I have compassion for these people; they have already been with me three days and have nothing to eat. I do not want to send them away hungry, or they may collapse on the way."

IMAGININGS

His disciples answered, "Where could we get enough bread in this remote place to feed such a crowd?"

"How many loaves do you have?" Jesus asked.

"Seven," they replied, "and a few small fish."

He told the crowd to sit down on the ground. Then he took the seven loaves and the fish, and when he had given thanks, he broke them and gave them to the disciples, and they in turn to the people. They all ate and were satisfied. Afterward the disciples picked up seven basketfuls of broken pieces that were left over. The number of those who ate was four thousand men, besides women and children.

Matthew 15:32-38

~ ~ ~ ~ ~

As evening approached, the disciples came to him and said, "This is a remote place, and it's already getting late. Send the crowds away, so they can go to the villages and buy themselves some food."

Jesus replied, "They do not need to go away. You give them something to eat."

"We have here only five loaves of bread and two fish," they answered.

"Bring them here to me," he said. And he directed the people to sit down on the grass. Taking the five loaves and the two fish and looking up to heaven, he gave thanks and broke the loaves. Then he gave them to the disciples, and the disciples gave them to the people. They all ate and were satisfied, and the disciples picked up twelve basketfuls of broken pieces that were left over. The number of those who ate was about five thousand men, besides women and children.

Matthew 14:15-21

~ ~ ~ ~ ~

IMAGININGS

Simon Peter said, "I'm going fishing."

"We'll come, too," they all said. So they went out in the boat, but they caught nothing all night.

At dawn Jesus was standing on the beach, but the disciples couldn't see who he was. He called out, "Fellows, have you caught any fish?"

"No," they replied.

Then he said, "Throw out your net on the right-hand side of the boat, and you'll get some!" So they did, and they couldn't haul in the net because there were so many fish in it.

John 21:3-6

~ ~ ~ ~ ~

IMAGINE

"Jonah was in the belly of the fish three days and three nights." – Jonah 1:17

"Take the first fish you catch; open its mouth and you will find a four-drachma coin." – Matthew 17:27

"We have here only five loaves of bread and two fish." – Matthew 14:17

"They couldn't haul in the net because there were so many fish in it." – John 21:6

~ ~ ~ ~ ~

All the fish mentioned in the Bible got together to swap stories. The biggest fish in the room spoke first: "Some preachers give me indigestion. I'll never forget the day I was cruising along beneath the stormy waves of the

Mediterranean Sea, when this delicious looking morsel, Jonah, began thrashing around after landing on the waves with a splat. He was just the right size for my afternoon snack, so I swallowed him whole. The guy resisted my stomach acid and for three days kept stomping around in my stomach, complaining. He didn't even have the courtesy to remove his sandals, and I think I got an ulcer from his constant pacing. He kept crawling up to my gills and clawing; every time he stood up, his head knocked the air out of my swim bladder. To say the least this preacher was hard to stomach, and it took him three days to start praying. I can't tell you how happy that made me because I had been praying ever since I swallowed him. The first time I came to shallow water, I regurgitated him onto the beach. If the guy had prayed when he first hit the water, he could have saved us both a lot of time and trouble.

Next up was the richest fish in the room. Every time someone wanted a soft drink, this fish would grin and spit out change for the vending machine. He spoke with pride about how Jesus had used him to teach a lesson about paying taxes. It seems Jesus told Peter to go catch a fish and reach into its mouth, where he would find a four-drachma coin, which he should use to pay both his and Jesus' taxes. Another fish asked what they were supposed to learn from that story, and the rich fish gave a dramatic answer. He opened his mouth and began to spit out pesos, euros, rupees, liras, drachmas, and centavos. With a sly grin he asked, "Why do humans worry so about this stuff when God makes it every day?"

Next to speak was a little dried sardine, who shared how God used him and his six brothers to feed four thousand humans. "Surely," said the sardine, "this must have been God's most impressive miracle, and he used me to do it!" A shy sardine spoke from the back of the room, "It was a great miracle all right, but you need to be careful about labeling your miracle as 'God's greatest.' God always has an even greater miracle waiting right around the corner. There were only two of us sardines that day when Jesus decided to use us to feed five thousand people. I once thought I was God's greatest miracle, but having witnessed so many miracles in my life, I've decided to quit limiting God."

The meeting closed when the fish choir took the stage to sing. There were so many of them, the risers began to break. A couple of the bigger choir members stepped off the risers and laughed, "We remember the time we were gathered for fish choir practice over on the safe side of the fisherman's boat. Since fishermen throw their nets from right to left we gathered on the other side of the boat so our choir practice would not be disturbed. You could have knocked us over with a mackerel when the net came down on the wrong side of the boat, capturing the entire choir. When the humans hoisted us into their boats, the nets began breaking just like the risers did today. Since that day, we've come to understand that God hangs out on both sides of the boat.

~ ~ ~ ~ ~

FOOD FOR THOUGHT

Why did Jonah wait three days in the fish's belly before he prayed (Jonah 2:7)?

What was the point of Jesus getting tax money from the mouth of a fish?

In what ways do we limit God by characterizing his past achievements as His "greatest"?

What did the fishermen learn when they cast their nets on the other side of the boat? How might that lesson apply to your life or to your church?

~ ~ ~ ~ ~

SHARING IT WITH GOD

Great God of the land and the sea, remind me to pray before I've sunk to the bottom. Lessen my trust in money, and increase my trust in the Creator of wealth. Help me to remember how easily you fed the masses with such meager supplies. Break my nets as I obey your Word. Amen.

~ ~ ~ ~ ~

BIRD BRAINS

Scripture

Therefore I tell you, do not worry about your life, what you will eat; or about your body, what you will wear. For life is more than food, and the body more than clothes. Consider the ravens: They do not sow or reap, they have no storeroom or barn; yet God feeds them. And how much more valuable you are than birds! Who of you by worrying can add a single hour to your life? Since you cannot do this very little thing, why do you worry about the rest?

Consider how the wild flowers grow. They do not labor or spin. Yet I tell you, not even Solomon in all his splendor was dressed like one of these. If that is how God clothes the grass of the field, which is here today, and tomorrow is thrown into the fire, how much more will he clothe you—you of little faith! And do not set your heart on what you will eat or drink; do not worry about it. For the pagan world runs after all such things, and your Father knows that you need them. But seek his kingdom, and these things will be given to you as well.

Luke 12:22-31

~ ~ ~ ~ ~

IMAGINE

"Therefore I tell you, do not worry about your life, what you will eat; or about your body, what you will wear." – Luke 12:22

"Consider the ravens." – Luke 12:24

"Consider how the wild flowers grow." – Luke 12:27a

~ ~ ~ ~ ~

It was the *National Bird Symposium on Anxiety,* and they were all there: stressed scissortails, worried warblers, depressed ducks, migrained mallards, harassed herons, neurotic nightingales, bulimic blackbirds, anorexic albatrosses, quivering quail, frantic finches, distressed doves, concerned cuckoos, foreboding flamingoes, jittery jays, panicky pelicans, shivering swifts, and troubled toucans. They were anxiously perched on the backs of their seats awaiting the keynote speech addressing this year's theme, *"The Coming Worm Shortage."*

It was a pitiful sight, with all those symptoms of anxiety dripping from the gathering of fowl like a roomful of leaky faucets at a plumber's convention. There was the naked buzzard, whose feathers had all fallen out from worry that here might be a carcass shortage. There was the tense turkey, whose nerves were on edge from worry over the anticipated decline in bugs. There was the ulcer-prone crow, nervously pecking at a box of antacids as his stomach burned for fear there would be nothing to steal from the other birds. The bird droppings from nervous fowl were so copious the aviary was about to become uninhabitable.

Finally, to everyone's relief, the head heron took the stage, only to belatedly announce the keynote speaker had decided to go look for worms rather than give his speech. In his place they were honored to hear from the wise old owl. When all the chirping, cackling, and crowing stopped, the owl spoke. "The coming worm shortage may or may not be a fact. It doesn't matter. Remember last year when there weren't as many worms as the previous year but there was an increase in insects? Remember the year of the great snow, and we couldn't see the bare ground for six weeks but not one of us starved to death? Let us not forget why God put us here—to encourage the faith of these humans, who worry about all these things. Our calling is to sing our songs and find our food where God has hidden it and in so doing bring hope to the forgetful humans."

With those words, the owl flew off to his next speaking appointment at the *National Symposium of Laid-back Lilies.* There the topic for the year was, *"Whatever Will We Wear This Spring?"* Rumor had it that there was great anxiety among the lilies over the fact they were nothing but bulbs today and they had no experience that would enable them to become beautiful tomorrow. The owl pulled out his notes from the bird symposium, changed the nouns from "birds" to "flowers," and gave the same speech.

Every human who obsesses over economic indicators would do well to take up bird watching and leaf peeping. At least Jesus seemed to think so.

~ ~ ~ ~ ~

FOOD FOR THOUGHT

What are the greatest worries of people today?

How should we apply Jesus' admonition not to worry?

IMAGININGS

How might nature study affect one's faith?

Is receiving the necessities of life from God contingent upon our putting his kingdom first?

~ ~ ~ ~ ~

SHARING IT WITH GOD

Generous God who has given me everything that pertains to life, raise my awareness that all I have comes from you. Help me not to trust in my own ability to provide for myself but to lean on you for all my needs. May I never forget the obvious evidences of your loving concern for me demonstrated in nature. Amen.

~ ~ ~ ~ ~

A TALE OF TWO PROPHETS

Scripture

In the year that King Uzziah died, I saw the Lord, high and exalted, seated on a throne; and the train of his robe filled the temple. Above him were seraphim, each with six wings: With two wings they covered their faces, with two they covered their feet, and with two they were flying. And they were calling to one another:

"Holy, holy, holy is the LORD Almighty;
the whole earth is full of his glory."

At the sound of their voices the doorposts and thresholds shook and the temple was filled with smoke.

"Woe to me!" I cried. "I am ruined! For I am a man of unclean lips, and I live among a people of unclean lips, and my eyes have seen the King, the LORD Almighty."

Then one of the seraphim flew to me with a live coal in his hand, which he had taken with tongs from the altar. With it he touched my mouth and said, "See, this has touched your lips; your guilt is taken away and your sin atoned for."

Then I heard the voice of the Lord saying, "Whom shall I send? And who will go for us?"

And I said, "Here am I. Send me!"

Isaiah 6:1-8

~ ~ ~ ~ ~

The word of the LORD came to Jonah son of Amittai: "Go to the great city of Nineveh and preach against it, because its wickedness has come up before me."

But Jonah ran away from the LORD and headed for Tarshish. He went down to Joppa, where he found a ship bound for that port. After paying the fare, he went aboard and sailed for Tarshish to flee from the LORD.

Jonah 1:1-3

~ ~ ~ ~ ~

IMAGINE

"Here am I; send me!" – Isaiah 6:8

"Jonah set out to flee . . ." – Jonah 1:3

~ ~ ~ ~ ~

It was the annual convention of prophets, and they were all there: Elijah, Daniel, Jeremiah, Elisha, Isaiah, Jonah, Amos, Hosea, Joel, Obadiah, Micah, Nahum, Habakkuk, Zephaniah, Malachi, Haggai, Ezekiel, and Zechariah. One of the favorite parts of the conference were the breakout sessions, when the prophets would pair off for one-on-one, "How's your ministry going?" sessions. At the 10:00 A.M. break, Isaiah and Jonah chatted over a plate of manna and quail appetizers.

IMAGININGS

Jonah loved the annual conference. When he left the conference, he always felt a special sense of closeness to God after talking about religion for days on end. Here he was sitting at the table with none other than the fantastic Isaiah. What a moment! He looked around for someone to take a picture of him chatting with Isaiah. He planned on getting Isaiah to sign the picture, and then having it enlarged, framed, and hung in his office.

Jonah began the conversation by asking Isaiah what motivated him to become a prophet. Isaiah spoke of being drawn to the incredible holiness of God in a vision he had years ago. "It was from that vision that I began to see myself as God's partner in evangelism. As I listened to the voice of God, it was painfully obvious he was limiting himself to the cooperative assistance of men who were willing to take his message anywhere and everywhere. The more I shared God's message with others, the clearer my view of the coming Messiah became. Ultimately, I came to see the coming Messiah as a servant willing to suffer anything to communicate the grace of God to lost people. That message was so important to me that I was willing to be sawn in half rather than recant."

Jonah was embarrassed and speechless. Isaiah encouraged him to share his story. Contritely, Jonah began his story. "I'm embarrassed to say that I had never thought about God's love for all people, so when God told me to go preach to a bunch of undeserving Gentiles in Nineveh, I rebelled. Little did I know the depths to which my racism would drag me, but I found myself sitting in the belly of a fish at the bottom of the sea. It took three days for me to come to my senses and agree to do what God had commanded. When I finally ended my poor man's ocean voyage, I dragged my feet into Nineveh, preached a partial message to one-third of the people, and, to my shock, the entire city repented. I cannot tell you how ashamed I am at how I reacted to God's forgiving my enemies, the Ninevites. I got mad at God for being full of grace. It took me quite a while to discover that were it not for the grace of God, I never would have gotten out of the fish's belly, never would have survived the storm on the sea, and for that matter never would have had any hope of heaven. In my life I ran from God and ahead of God, but I finally started running with him."

~ ~ ~ ~ ~

FOOD FOR THOUGHT

What motivated Isaiah to answer God's call in Isaiah 6?

What kept Jonah from answering God's call?

What made Jonah think he could sail away from God?

How does seeing God's holiness and grace draw people to him?

~ ~ ~ ~ ~

SHARING IT WITH GOD

God who calls me to take his message to others, influence my words so that they reflect your concern for the lost. Keep me from the temptation to judge others as unworthy of your forgiveness. Instill in my heart the same passion for the lost that your Son had. May I never take grace for granted. Amen.

~ ~ ~ ~ ~

BENT OUT OF SHAPE

SCRIPTURE

On a Sabbath Jesus was teaching in one of the synagogues, and a woman was there whom a spirit had crippled for eighteen years. She was bent over and could not straighten up at all. When Jesus saw her, he called her forward and said to her, "Woman, you are set free from your infirmity." Then he put his hands on her, and immediately she straightened up and praised God.

Indignant because Jesus had healed on the Sabbath, the synagogue leader said to the people, "There are six days for work. So come and be healed on those days, not on the Sabbath."

The Lord answered him, "You hypocrites! Doesn't each of you on the Sabbath untie your ox or donkey from the stall and lead it out to give it water? Then should not this woman, a daughter of Abraham, whom Satan has kept bound for eighteen long years, be set free on the Sabbath day from what bound her?"

When he said this, all his opponents were humiliated, but the people were delighted with all the wonderful things he was doing.

Luke 13:10-17

~ ~ ~ ~ ~

IMAGINE

"She was bent over and was quite unable to stand up straight." – Luke 13:11

"She stood up straight and began praising God." – Luke 13:13

"There are six days on which work ought to be done; come on those

days and be cured, and not on the Sabbath day." – Luke 13:14

~ ~ ~ ~ ~

She awakened to the ritual crowing of the rooster and began the slow, painful process of uncurling her body from the fetal position in which she was forced to sleep. Eventually she was able to stand, though her bent-over body refused to straighten up. Over the course of eighteen years, her back had become more and more hunched over. She put on her clothing and shuffled her way out the door, heading for the synagogue as she did every Saturday. She rarely went anywhere because walking was painful, but she was determined to continue traipsing to synagogue as long as her stooped body could endure the journey.

She shuffled into the synagogue, taking the first seat available near the back. A few people spoke to her, but she couldn't raise her head enough to recognize them. She heard the voice of a new teacher, but she didn't know who he was because she couldn't see above the waist of the woman seated in front of her. She was shocked when the teacher called her to come to him. She plodded her way to the front of the synagogue and stood there, stooped over, staring at the teacher's feet. His words were commanding, "Woman, you are set free from your ailment!" For a moment she wondered if there was any power in his words; but then he touched her, and immediately she stood straight and tall, looking directly into the eyes of the Great Physician. For the first time in eighteen years, she looked up into heaven as she shouted her praise to God.

She was not the only deformed person in the synagogue that day. If she was deformed physically, the leader of the synagogue was deformed spiritually. His indignant words shocked the crowd like cold ice water thrown on an unsuspecting victim: *"There are six days on which work ought to be done; come on those days and be cured, and not on the Sabbath day."* She felt chastised by his words as she found her spirit of praise being quenched by guilt. But before the synagogue ruler could impose his own curvature of the spirit on the woman's soul, Jesus silenced the ruler's legalism with the words, *"You hypocrites!"*

Two people were bent out of shape that Sabbath day in the synagogue. An evil spirit bent one out of shape physically; a legalistic spirit bent the other out of shape. Only one received healing.

~ ~ ~ ~ ~

FOOD FOR THOUGHT

What are some characteristics of people who come to church feeling like the bent-over woman?

What did the ruler of the synagogue misunderstand about the Sabbath law he quoted?

What are people to do if they find themselves with a set of rules longer than God's?

What evidence is there in the text that the woman's grateful spirit was contagious?

What evidence is there in the text that the ruler's legalistic spirit was contagious?

~ ~ ~ ~ ~

SHARING IT WITH GOD

God who can make crooked paths straight, guard my spirit from thinking rules are more important than people. May the same compassion that characterized your Son characterize me. May the same gratitude that filled the healed woman's spirit fill my spirit. Enable me to see the hurting people in this world who have become invisible to others. Amen.

~ ~ ~ ~ ~

EPILOGUE

Long ago King David hinted at how he composed much of the Jewish hymnal we know as the book of *Psalms*. He said he meditated on God's law day and night. It is one thing to read the Scriptures. It is quite another to meditate on them. To meditate on Scripture is not to merely think about the text but to pose questions to the text.

It was the task of the Holy Spirit to inspire the Scriptures. With the Spirit's help, it is the task of the Bible student to illuminate the Scriptures. Illumination is the product of imagination. IMAGINE!

www.ingramcontent.com/pod-product-compliance
Ingram Content Group UK Ltd.
Pitfield, Milton Keynes, MK11 3LW, UK
UKHW041948230426
12048UKWH00008B/210